HOW TO OPEN A
JEWELRY STORE

A Comprehensive Guide to Starting, Running and
Growing Your Own Jewelry Retailing Business

MORRIS WILLIS

TABLE OF CONTENTS

Introduction

In a world where first impressions count and personal style speaks volumes, the jewelry we adorn ourselves with becomes a canvas for our individuality, aspirations, and even our emotions. Jewelry isn't merely an accessory; it's a form of self-expression, a source of beauty, and a symbol of our unique identity. This fusion of artistry and personal significance is what propels the enduring allure of jewelry, shaping an industry that's forever evolving and captivating.

Welcome to the gateway of this vibrant and dynamic realm of retail. Whether you're a seasoned jewelry enthusiast yearning to transform your passion into a business or an aspiring entrepreneur seeking a niche in the competitive jewelry market, this guide is tailored to furnish you with the essential knowledge, skills, and strategies required to thrive in the jewelry retail sphere.

From deciphering market trends and conducting comprehensive market research to handpicking the ideal location, curating the perfect inventory, and crafting a distinct brand identity, this book navigates you through each pivotal stage on your voyage toward owning and managing a flourishing jewelry store.

Within the upcoming chapters, we'll delve into legal and financial considerations, explore the artistry of branding and store aesthetics, and unravel the intricacies of inventory management, staffing, and delivering exceptional customer service. We'll also navigate through the labyrinth of marketing techniques and the expanding horizons of e-commerce. Moreover, we'll address the hurdles that accompany running a jewelry store and furnish pragmatic solutions to overcome them.

Establishing a jewelry store transcends merely unlocking doors; it's about offering patrons quality, elegance, and a touch of personality through their accessories. It's about sculpting a brand that resonates deeply within your community and fashioning a shopping experience that beckons customers time and again. It's about embarking on an entrepreneurial journey where each stride is as significant as the last.

Thus, whether you're on the brink of inaugurating your inaugural jewelry store or refining an existing venture, this guide will stand as your steadfast companion, furnishing insights, best practices, and real-world wisdom to guide you confidently into the world of jewelry retail and onward toward triumph.

Let us embark on this odyssey of crafting a jewelry store that etches an enduring mark, one adornment at a time.

Chapter 1:
The Allure of the Jewelry Business

Jewelry isn't just about looking pretty; it's got this incredible pull that goes deeper than what meets the eye. They are emotional anchors, carrying memories and cultural meanings that stretch back through time. It's about connecting with emotions, celebrating milestones, and making memories. Ever put on a piece that's been in your family for generations? That kind of jewelry carries the weight of history and love, right there on your wrist or around your neck.

And let's not forget the skill, the patience, and the creativity that go into making each piece! It's like an art form in itself. Across the ages, artisans have poured their hearts into these creations, from the ancient symbols to the cutting-edge designs we see today. When you comprehend the skill, dedication, and creativity poured into these creations, it helps you curate a collection that reflects that passion. As a jewelry store owner, knowing and valuing this craftsmanship sets your store apart—it's not just about selling jewelry; it's about showcasing art. It's about empowering people to express themselves through the jewelry they wear.

But it's not all about looks or craftsmanship. Jewelry also has this way of saying something about who you are. It's not just about showing off wealth or status anymore; it's about expressing yourself. The pieces you choose? They're a glimpse into your style, your beliefs, and what matters to you.

So, as a jewelry store owner, comprehending the multifaceted allure of jewelry isn't just a nice-to-have—it's a necessity. It's about knowing your product at its core, connecting with your customers' emotions, respecting the craftsmanship, and providing a space for personal expression. This understanding becomes the foundation for creating a store that's not just about selling jewelry but about being a part of people's stories.

Why Open a Jewelry Store

Opening a jewelry store offers an incredible chance to dive into a world that's not just about selling items but creating connections and marking special moments in people's lives.

One awesome thing about running a jewelry store is that you're involved in some of the most meaningful events in people's lives, like engagements, weddings, or milestone celebrations. Being a part of those moments and helping customers find or create pieces that hold deep sentimental value is incredibly rewarding.

Plus, a jewelry store is a hub where cultural traditions and creativity collide. You have the chance to preserve and celebrate diverse cultural heritages through the jewelry you offer. Whether it's showcasing pieces that reflect various traditions or coming up with new designs inspired by these rich cultures, it's a platform for sharing and appreciating heritage.

On the business side, running a jewelry store can also be quite profitable. Quality jewelry tends to hold its value, and building a reputation for offering top-notch pieces and great service can attract loyal customers. Jewelry, when treated with expertise and care, can also be seen as an investment, both for your store and the customers buying from you.

Another exciting aspect is the ever-evolving nature of the jewelry industry. Trends in design, materials, and what customers like are always changing. This allows for a dynamic and exciting environment where you can constantly adapt, introduce new collections, and explore innovative designs to keep up with evolving tastes.

Ultimately, opening a jewelry store is about becoming a part of people's stories, preserving cultural legacies, and building a business that celebrates beauty, craftsmanship, and emotion. It's a chance to connect with customers on a personal level and be a part of their cherished moments while also running a business that can be both emotionally fulfilling and profitable.

Choosing Your Niche

When it comes to jewelry stores, there's a whole spectrum of specialties and niches. Deciding where you fit in this diverse landscape is crucial.

First off, you've got your traditional fine jewelry stores. These places specialize in high-end pieces—diamonds, precious gemstones, and top-notch craftsmanship. They're all about luxury, elegance, and timeless designs. Think engagement rings, stunning necklaces, and heirloom-quality pieces.

Then, there are contemporary or fashion-forward jewelry stores. They're more about trendy designs, experimenting with materials, and appealing to a younger or more fashion-conscious crowd. You'll find pieces that follow current trends, use alternative materials, or focus on unique, statement-making designs.

If vintage is your thing, there's a niche for that too. Vintage or antique jewelry stores deal in pieces from bygone eras, offering a sense of nostalgia and history. They often have unique and rare finds, appealing to collectors or those seeking something with a story behind it.

Another interesting niche is artisanal or handmade jewelry stores. These places highlight the craftsmanship of independent designers or local artisans. They're all about unique, one-of-a-kind pieces that showcase creativity and individuality. Customers drawn to authenticity and supporting artisans often flock to these stores.

And let's not forget about specialized stores like those focusing on specific types of jewelry—be it custom-made pieces, eco-friendly materials, or jewelry catering to a particular cultural aesthetic.

Deciding your niche involves understanding your strengths, your target audience, and what sets you apart. Maybe you have a passion for sustainable materials or a knack for modern, edgy designs. Perhaps you want to specialize in rare gemstones or cater to a specific cultural style. Whatever it is, finding your unique angle in the jewelry world can help you stand out and attract the right clientele.

Chapter 2:
Market Research and Planning

In business, the adage "knowledge is power" rings especially true. Prior to stepping into the realm of launching your own jewelry store, it's imperative to equip yourself with comprehensive insights into your market and a meticulously crafted strategy. This section lays the foundation for your jewelry store endeavor, focusing on four pivotal elements: Understanding Your Customer Base, Selecting the Right Location, Analyzing Competition, and Crafting a Business Blueprint.

Understanding Your Target Market

An essential pillar for success in the jewelry retail business hinges upon deeply understanding your target market. The ability to meet your customers' needs, preferences, and aspirations is pivotal in cultivating a thriving jewelry store. Here, we'll delve into the steps aimed at comprehending your target market and tailoring your jewelry collection to specifically meet their demands.

Commence by defining the demographics of your ideal customer base. This includes factors like age, gender, income, occupation, and location. For instance, if your store is situated near a university, your target market might consist of young adults seeking trendy yet affordable jewelry. Conversely, in a business district, your focus might shift to working professionals desiring sophisticated and elegant pieces.

Dive deeper into understanding your customers' lifestyles, values, and interests. Do they prioritize sustainable and ethical jewelry? Are they fashion-forward trendsetters or individuals valuing comfort and enduring style? Grasping these elements aids in curating your jewelry assortment in alignment with their values and tastes.

Analyze your customers' purchasing behavior. Are they spontaneous buyers, or do they meticulously research their jewelry acquisitions? Do they prefer in-store shopping experiences or lean towards online purchases? Recognizing these traits assists in tailoring marketing strategies and enhancing the overall customer journey.

Different customers seek distinct types of jewelry. Some might be inclined towards statement pieces, while others seek delicate, everyday wear. Understanding these preferences enables you to offer the right variety of jewelry items. Also, acknowledge how seasonal changes impact your customers' jewelry needs. Festive seasons, weddings, or holidays often drive specific jewelry demands. Adapting your inventory and marketing strategies accordingly is vital.

Explore your competitors to comprehend their customer base and discern what sets your jewelry store apart. This aids in identifying untapped niches or areas where you can provide a unique value proposition.

Regularly gather feedback from your customers through surveys, online reviews, or direct interactions. Listening to their perspectives and addressing their needs not only enhances your offerings but also fosters customer loyalty. Stay abreast of industry trends and market research. Consumer preferences evolve, and staying informed allows you to adapt and stay ahead in the competitive landscape.

By comprehensively understanding your target market, you can refine your jewelry collection, marketing endeavors, and store ambiance to cater precisely to their desires. For example, if your research unveils a preference for ethically sourced jewelry among your clientele, considering sustainable jewelry brands could be a strategic move. Similarly, offering convenient online shopping options could cater to customers valuing ease and efficiency.

Keep in mind that your target market may evolve, necessitating adjustments in your strategies. Continuously assessing and adapting your approach ensures your jewelry store remains relevant and appealing, fostering enduring success.

Choosing the Right Location

Once you've nailed down your target market, the next critical move is pinpointing the perfect location for your jewelry store. Your store's location isn't merely its address; it's a strategic choice that can define your brand, attract customers, and impact your financial performance. Here, we'll delve into key considerations to guide your decision in choosing the ideal location for your jewelry store.

Optimal visibility and easy accessibility are paramount. Aim for locations with high foot traffic, ideally near residential areas. Such visibility and accessibility increase the likelihood of potential customers discovering your store. A well-situated store captures attention and invites passersby to explore your collection.

Research the competitive landscape in your selected area. Are there established jewelry stores nearby? Understanding competitors helps you carve out a unique position. It may also unveil untapped market segments your store can effectively cater to.

Align the location with your target customers' demographics and preferences. Different neighborhoods attract varying customer profiles and buying behaviors. For instance, a location near a college might appeal to younger adults seeking trendy, affordable jewelry, while a family-centric area might prioritize convenience for parents and kids.

Complying with local zoning regulations and permits is crucial. These regulations influence store operations, from layout to product offerings. Being aware and compliant with local laws avoids legal issues down the line.

Financial considerations are pivotal. Evaluate expenses like rent, utilities, and ongoing maintenance against your budget. Ensuring the location aligns with your financial capabilities is vital for a favorable return on investment.

Choosing your jewelry store's location is a multifaceted decision that demands careful analysis. It's more than just a physical space; it's a strategic asset shaping your business success. By focusing on visibility, competition, demographics, regulations, and costs, you can make an informed decision positioning your jewelry store for success in the competitive retail world. The right location can drive foot traffic, distinguish you from competitors, and forge strong connections with your target market, contributing to your store's growth and prosperity.

Competitive Analysis

Knowing your competition is crucial for making your jewelry store stand out in the market. To do this well, take a deep dive into your competitors' strengths, weaknesses, opportunities, and threats through a comprehensive analysis. Here's how you can approach this for your jewelry store:

Start by making a list of all the other jewelry stores in your area. But don't stop at just direct competitors. Consider nearby boutiques, online jewelry sellers, and big retail chains that might draw a similar crowd. The wider your scope, the better your understanding will be.

For each competitor, do a SWOT analysis. Look at what they're good at, like unique designs or strong branding. Also, spot their weaknesses, such as limited variety or outdated ways of doing things. Check out the opportunities they might be missing, like reaching out to certain types of customers or keeping up with new jewelry trends. Finally, figure out the threats they face, such as new stores opening up or changes in what customers want. This analysis helps you see where you stand in the market.

Now, figure out what makes your jewelry store special. What's your Unique Selling Proposition (USP)? It could be something like offering custom designs, using ethically sourced materials, or providing a personalized shopping experience. Your USP is what makes customers want to choose your store.

Look into how your competitors set their prices. Some might focus on luxury while others aim for more affordable options. Your pricing should match your customers' preferences and fit with your USP. It's a balancing act between being competitive and making a profit.

If you can, get info on how much of the market each competitor has. This helps you see who's the big player and where there might be room for you to shine. Even if a competitor seems strong, there might still be areas where they're not meeting customers' needs.

Analyzing your competition is like making a map for your jewelry store's success. It shows you where the opportunities are and helps you figure out how to stand out. By really understanding what your competitors are good at and where they fall short, you can make smart choices for your jewelry store and set yourself up for success in a competitive market.

Crafting a Comprehensive Business Plan

Now that you've grasped the ins and outs of your target market, secured an optimal location, and gained insights into your competition, it's time to weave this valuable information into a structured business plan. Your business plan acts as the roadmap guiding your jewelry store toward triumph. It encompasses several key components, each contributing to the overarching framework of your vision:

Executive Summary: Leading your business plan is the executive summary. This concise segment encapsulates your business's core, featuring your mission statement, overarching objectives, and a summary of your financial forecasts.

Company Description: Delve deeply into your jewelry store's intricacies within the company description section. Paint a vivid picture of your venture, elucidating your vision, the array of products you plan to offer, your unique selling propositions, and a profile of your target market.

Market Analysis: Summarize the insights gleaned from exhaustive market research. Include crucial details about your target market's demographics, the strategic selection of your location, and the competitive landscape you've uncovered.

Organization and Management: Offer an organizational blueprint. Who comprises your key team members, and what roles will they fulfill? Highlight relevant experience and qualifications that strengthen your team's ability to execute your business strategy.

Products and Services: Outline a comprehensive list of the products and services your jewelry store will provide. Elaborate on any distinctive or specialty items in your inventory and clarify your sourcing strategy.

Sales and Marketing: Detail your sales and marketing strategies. How will you allure and retain customers? Explain your advertising campaigns, promotional tactics, and the channels you'll use to effectively reach your audience.

Funding Request: If you're seeking external financing, articulate your funding needs. Specify precisely how you intend to allocate these funds and outline the terms you're seeking from potential investors or lenders.

Financial Projections: Support your plan with meticulous financial projections. Include comprehensive income statements, balance sheets, and cash flow statements spanning at least three to five years. These projections offer a tangible picture of your financial trajectory.

Appendix: Compile supplementary documents that strengthen your business plan. This might encompass market research data, resumes showcasing key team members' expertise, and essential supplier agreements.

Remember that your business plan isn't a static document; it should evolve alongside your business. It serves as a dynamic tool for strategizing, decision-making, and effectively conveying your vision to potential investors and stakeholders. With a robust business plan in hand, you'll be better equipped to navigate the dynamic jewelry store landscape and steer your venture toward long-term success.

Chapter 3:
Legal and Regulatory Considerations

Starting and operating a jewelry store involves navigating a complex web of legal and regulatory requirements. Understanding and complying with these rules is essential to ensure the smooth and legal operation of your business. In this chapter, we'll explore the key legal and regulatory considerations for your jewelry store, including choosing the right business structure, obtaining permits and licenses, adhering to health and safety regulations, and managing taxation.

Choosing a Business Structure

One of the first decisions you'll need to make when starting your jewelry store is choosing the right business structure. The structure you select will have implications for your personal liability, taxation, and how you can raise capital. Here are some common business structures to consider:

Sole Proprietorship: This is the simplest and most common form of business ownership. As a sole proprietor, you have complete control over your jewelry store, but you are personally responsible for all business debts and liabilities. Your business income and expenses are reported on your personal tax return.

Partnership: If you plan to start your jewelry store with one or more partners, a partnership structure may be suitable. Partnerships can be general partnerships (where partners share equally in profits and liabilities) or limited partnerships (where some partners have limited liability). Like sole proprietors, partners report their share of business income and expenses on their personal tax returns.

Limited Liability Company (LLC): An LLC provides a level of personal liability protection for its owners (called members). Members are typically not personally responsible for the company's debts and liabilities. LLCs offer flexibility in management and taxation, as they can be taxed as a sole proprietorship, partnership, or corporation.

Corporation: A corporation is a separate legal entity from its owners (shareholders). This structure offers the most significant personal liability protection, as shareholders are generally not personally liable for the company's debts. Corporations also have the advantage of attracting outside investors by issuing shares of stock. However, corporations have more complex tax and regulatory requirements.

Choosing the right business structure is a critical decision that should align with your long-term goals and financial considerations. Consult with legal and financial advisors to assess the best option for your jewelry store.

Permits and Licenses

Running a jewelry store requires various permits and licenses to comply with local, state, and federal regulations. These licenses and permits demonstrate that your store meets specific health, safety, and operational standards. Here's an overview of the essential permits and licenses you may need:

Business License: Most cities or municipalities require businesses to obtain a general business license. This license allows you to operate legally within a specific jurisdiction. The requirements and fees for business licenses vary by location.

Alcohol License: If you plan to sell alcoholic beverages in your jewelry store, you'll need an alcohol license. These licenses are highly regulated and often require adherence to specific rules regarding sales, hours of operation, and age restrictions.

Building and Zoning Permits: Before you open your store or make significant renovations, you'll need building and zoning permits to ensure that your physical location complies with local building codes and zoning regulations.

Signage Permit: Some municipalities have specific rules regarding outdoor signage. You may need a signage permit to display your store's name, logo, and advertising.

Fire Department Permits: Fire departments may require permits for fire safety, particularly if you store flammable materials or have specific fire prevention measures in place.

Tobacco Retailer License: If you plan to sell tobacco products, you may need a tobacco retailer license, which regulates the sale of cigarettes, cigars, and other tobacco items.

Specialty Permits: Depending on the unique features of your jewelry store, you may require additional permits. For example, if you plan to host live music or events, you may need an entertainment permit.

It's essential to research and identify the specific permits and licenses required in your jurisdiction. Failure to obtain the necessary permits can result in fines, legal consequences, or the closure of your store. Local government websites and business development offices are valuable resources for information on required permits and licenses.

Taxation

Understanding the taxation aspects of your jewelry store is crucial for managing your finances and complying with tax laws. Here are key tax considerations:

Sales Tax: Most states and local jurisdictions impose sales tax on the sale of tangible goods, including jewelries. You are responsible for collecting and remitting sales tax to the appropriate taxing authorities. It's essential to understand the specific tax rates and exemptions that apply to jewelry items in your area.

Income Tax: Your jewelry store's income is subject to federal and state income taxes. The business structure you choose will determine how your income is taxed. Sole proprietors report business income on their personal tax returns, while corporations have separate tax obligations.

Employee Payroll Taxes: If you have employees, you must withhold and remit payroll taxes, including federal income tax, Social Security tax, and Medicare tax. Employers also pay a portion of these taxes.

Property Tax: Real property, such as the land and buildings housing your jewelry store, is subject to property tax. The amount of property tax you pay depends on the assessed value of your property and local tax rates.

Licensing and Permit Fees: Some licenses and permits may have associated fees that must be paid on a regular basis.

Use Tax: If your state imposes a use tax, you may be required to pay it on items purchased out of state for use in your business.

Business Deductions: Take advantage of tax deductions available to jewelry stores. These may include deductions for business expenses such as rent, utilities, advertising, and employee salaries.

Accounting and Recordkeeping: Maintain accurate financial records and accounting practices to facilitate tax compliance and reporting. Consider working with a certified public accountant (CPA) or tax professional to ensure accuracy.

Tax Credits and Incentives: Research if there are any tax credits or incentives available for jewelry stores in your region. Some areas offer incentives for businesses that promote healthy eating or invest in energy-efficient equipment.

Filing Deadlines: Familiarize yourself with tax filing deadlines and make sure you submit all required tax forms and payments on time to avoid penalties and interest.

Navigating the complexities of taxation can be challenging, so it's advisable to consult with a tax professional or CPA with experience in the retail and jewelry industry. They can help you maximize deductions, plan for tax liabilities, and ensure compliance with tax laws.

The legal and regulatory considerations for a jewelry store are multifaceted and demand meticulous attention. Choosing the right business structure, obtaining the necessary permits and licenses, adhering to health and safety regulations, and managing taxation are fundamental aspects of running a successful and legally compliant jewelry store. By investing the time and effort to understand and meet these requirements, you lay a solid foundation for the growth and longevity of your business.

Chapter 4:
Financing Your Jewelry Store

Financing is a critical aspect of launching and sustaining a successful jewelry store. In this chapter, we will explore the key elements of financing your jewelry store, including estimating startup costs, securing funding from various sources, and managing your finances effectively.

Estimating Startup Costs

Before opening the doors to your jewelry store, it's crucial to estimate and plan for the startup costs that will set your business in motion. This process involves meticulous financial planning to ensure that you have the necessary capital to cover initial expenses and establish a strong foundation for your new venture. Here's a breakdown of the key factors to consider when estimating your jewelry store's startup costs:

Location and Rent: The cost of securing the right location can vary significantly depending on factors like the size of the space, the area's desirability, and the local real estate market. Be prepared for the first month's rent and, if required, a security deposit.

Store Build-Out: Preparing your physical space for a jewelry store will involve costs for interior design, fixtures, shelving, lighting, flooring, and any necessary renovations. Ensure that the store layout complements your brand and enhances the shopping experience.

Inventory: Building up your initial jewelry inventory is one of the most substantial expenses. Your inventory should align with your target market and unique selling proposition. Consider factors like the variety of jewelry styles, sizes, and brands you want to offer.

Furniture and Equipment: You'll need furniture for your store, including chairs, tables, and possibly a checkout counter. Equipment such as cash registers, point-of-sale systems, security systems, and storage solutions will also require an investment.

Legal and Licensing Fees: Registering your business, obtaining permits, and complying with local regulations may entail legal and licensing fees. Consult with an attorney or a legal expert to navigate these requirements.

Branding and Marketing: Building your brand identity and marketing your jewelry store is essential for attracting customers. Expenses may include logo design, signage, promotional materials, and initial advertising campaigns.

Utilities and Overheads: Budget for utilities like electricity, water, and heating. Additionally, consider ongoing operating costs such as insurance, property taxes, and other overhead expenses.

Employee Wages: If you plan to hire staff, allocate funds for their wages and any training expenses. Remember to budget for employee benefits as well.

Technology and Software: Invest in the technology necessary for smooth store operations, including inventory management software, point-of-sale systems, and a website or e-commerce platform if you plan to sell online.

Miscellaneous Expenses: Anticipate miscellaneous costs, such as office supplies, initial inventory tracking software, and any unexpected expenses that may arise during the startup phase.

Working Capital: It's essential to have a reserve of working capital to cover expenses during the initial months when your business might not be generating substantial revenue.

Contingency Fund: Building in a contingency fund for unforeseen circumstances or unexpected costs is wise. This provides a safety net in case you encounter unexpected challenges.

To calculate a more accurate estimate of your startup costs, it's advisable to create a detailed business plan and financial projections. Seek the guidance of financial experts or accountants who can provide you with insights into the specific costs associated with starting a jewelry store. Additionally, exploring financing options, such as loans or investors, can help ensure you have the necessary capital to launch your business successfully.

Estimating your startup costs meticulously and being prepared for unexpected expenses is a critical step in the journey of opening a jewelry store. With a well-thought-out financial plan, you can confidently navigate the initial phase of your business and focus on providing exceptional jewelries and customer experiences to your patrons.

Securing Funding

Once you have a clear understanding of your startup costs, the next step is to secure the necessary funding. Financing your jewelry store may require a combination of personal savings, loans, investments, and grants. Here are some common sources of funding:

Personal Savings: Using your own savings to finance your jewelry store is a common and straightforward approach. It allows you to maintain full control of your business and eliminates the need to pay interest on loans.

Family and Friends: Some entrepreneurs turn to family members or close friends for financial support. While this can be an accessible source of funding, it's crucial to formalize any agreements in writing to avoid misunderstandings.

Small Business Loans: Banks and credit unions offer various types of small business loans, including term loans, lines of credit, and equipment financing. These loans often require a solid business plan and collateral.

SBA Loans: The U.S. Small Business Administration (SBA) provides loan programs to support small businesses. SBA loans typically have favorable terms and lower interest rates, but they also involve a rigorous application process.

Investors: Seek investors who are willing to provide capital in exchange for equity or a share of the profits. Angel investors, venture capitalists, and private equity firms are potential sources of investment.

Crowdfunding: Crowdfunding platforms, such as Kickstarter and Indiegogo, allow you to raise funds from a large number of people online. This method is particularly effective if you have a unique and compelling business concept.

Grants: Some government agencies, non-profit organizations, and foundations offer grants to support small businesses, especially those focused on community development or sustainable practices.

Supplier Financing: Negotiate favorable payment terms with your suppliers. Some suppliers may offer extended payment periods, allowing you to manage cash flow more effectively.

Franchise Opportunities: If you're considering opening a franchise jewelry store, the franchisor may provide financing options or assistance with securing loans.

Online Lenders: Online lending platforms offer various financing options, including short-term loans, business lines of credit, and invoice financing. These options may be more accessible for newer businesses.

Government Programs: Research local and state government programs that provide financial assistance, grants, or tax incentives to small businesses, especially those creating jobs or contributing to the local economy.

Alternative Funding: Explore alternative funding sources, such as merchant cash advances, factoring, or peer-to-peer lending. These options may be suitable for businesses with unique financing needs.

To secure funding successfully, you'll need to prepare a compelling business plan that demonstrates the viability and profitability of your jewelry store. Lenders and investors want to see that you have a clear vision, a solid market strategy, and a realistic financial forecast. Be prepared to provide financial statements, cash flow projections, and any collateral if required.

Managing Finances

Managing the finances of a jewelry business is crucial for its long-term success. It involves various essential practices to ensure effective financial control. Firstly, keeping accurate records of all financial transactions is key. This includes tracking income from events and expenses related to ingredients, equipment, staff wages, and other operational costs. Using reliable accounting software helps in keeping these records organized and precise.

Monitoring cash flow is another critical aspect. Catering businesses often experience fluctuations in income based on event bookings and seasonal demands. Therefore, keeping a close eye on money coming in and going out helps ensure there's enough cash to cover essential expenses, buy necessary supplies, pay employees, and manage unexpected costs. Creating cash flow projections assists in planning ahead for financial needs.

Crafting a detailed budget is essential. It should outline expected revenues and breakdown expenses, encompassing everything from ingredients and equipment to marketing and staffing costs. Regularly comparing the actual financial performance with the budget allows for adjustments to maintain financial stability.

Efficiently managing inventory is important too. Balancing inventory levels to meet demand without unnecessary stockpiling is crucial for financial health. Keeping an eye on stock levels and turnover rates helps in managing inventory effectively, minimizing waste, and maximizing profits.

Cost control is another significant aspect. Analyzing expenses and finding ways to reduce costs without compromising quality is vital. Negotiating better terms with suppliers, exploring bulk purchasing options, and optimizing staffing are effective strategies to manage costs.

Lastly, ensuring compliance with tax obligations, maintaining proper financial records, and regularly reviewing financial performance through reports like income statements and balance sheets are essential practices. Seeking advice from accountants or financial advisors specializing in the catering industry can offer valuable insights for making informed financial decisions and improving profitability. Managing finances in a catering business requires diligence and proactive strategies to ensure financial stability and support sustainable growth.

In conclusion, financing your jewelry store is a critical step in turning your business idea into reality. Estimating startup costs, securing funding from diverse sources, and implementing sound financial management practices are essential for the success and sustainability of your jewelry store. With careful planning and prudent financial management, you can build a thriving and financially resilient business.

Chapter 5:
Store Design and Layout

The design and layout of your jewelry store play a pivotal role in shaping the customer experience, optimizing efficiency, and driving sales. In this chapter, we will delve into the critical aspects of store design and layout, including store layout considerations, shelving and merchandising strategies, equipment and fixtures, and interior design.

Store Layout Considerations

Designing an effective store layout for a jewelry store requires thoughtful planning to craft a shopping environment that caters to your customers' needs while maximizing sales potential. Here are several key store layout considerations tailored to a jewelry retail setting:

Foot Traffic Flow: Commence by analyzing the natural flow of customer traffic within your jewelry store. Shoppers often follow a counterclockwise path, so it's prudent to design your layout to accommodate this pattern. Along this route, strategically position high-traffic jewelry displays and promotional areas to capture attention and stimulate purchases.

Aisles and Pathways: Ensure that your aisles are generously wide to facilitate easy navigation, especially for customers with shopping carts or strollers. Maintain consistent aisle widths throughout the store, with broader main aisles to accommodate heavy foot traffic.

Jewelry Grouping: Organize jewelries of similar styles or categories together to enhance the convenience of shopping for your customers. This simplifies the shopping process and encourages cross-selling opportunities.

Endcaps and Displays: Recognize the value of endcaps in your store. Utilize them to showcase featured jewelry collections, trendy jewelry, or special promotions. Eye-catching displays at the ends of aisles have the potential to capture shoppers' attention and encourage spontaneous purchases.

Checkout Placement: Position checkout counters strategically, typically near the front of the store, to entice last-minute purchases. Consider offering express lanes for customers with only a few pairs of jewelries, enhancing their shopping experience.

Store Entrance: Create an inviting store entrance with clear signage and well-maintained jewelry displays. Ensure that entering and exiting the store is straightforward for customers, with prominent signage guiding the way.

Store Lighting: Lighting is crucial for both aesthetics and visibility. Blend natural and artificial lighting to create a bright and welcoming atmosphere that showcases your jewelry collections effectively.

Planogram: Develop a planogram that precisely outlines the placement of jewelry products on shelves and displays. This visual guide guarantees consistency in product arrangement and maximizes product visibility.

Clear Signage: Employ clear and informative signage throughout the store to assist customers in locating specific jewelry styles. Signage should include aisle markers, product descriptions, and pricing information.

Accessibility: Make sure your jewelry store is accessible to all customers, including those with disabilities. Install ramps, handrails, and wider aisles to accommodate wheelchair users and individuals with mobility challenges.

Emergency Exits: Clearly mark emergency exits and maintain their accessibility at all times. Safety should always be a top priority in your jewelry store layout.

Restrooms and Amenities: If your store provides restroom facilities, position them near the entrance for easy access. Consider offering amenities like a water fountain or seating areas to enhance customer comfort.

Customer Service Counter: Position the customer service counter in proximity to the entrance or checkout area for efficient assistance with inquiries, returns, and other customer needs.

Storage and Backroom: Designate a well-organized storage and backroom area to facilitate efficient inventory management and restocking of jewelry products. Maintaining these areas in an organized manner ensures easy access to supplies and minimizes disruptions.

By carefully addressing these store layout considerations tailored to a jewelry store, you can create a shopping environment that not only meets your customers' expectations but also maximizes sales and elevates the overall jewelry-shopping experience.

Shelving and Merchandising

Efficient shelving and merchandising play a pivotal role in the art of presenting jewelry products attractively, maximizing space, and ultimately boosting sales. To achieve these objectives, consider incorporating the following strategies tailored to a jewelry store:

Begin by choosing the right shelving options that align with the specific needs of your jewelry store. Common choices include wall-mounted jewelry displays, floor-standing racks, and specialized shelving designed to showcase different jewelry categories. Customize the arrangement of your jewelry displays to accommodate the varying sizes and styles of jewelries you offer. Position lower shelves to showcase easily accessible jewelry options, while strategically placing eye-level displays to draw attention to high-end or newly arrived jewelries.

Implement effective visual merchandising by thoughtfully arranging jewelries on shelves. Highlight best-selling and high-margin jewelry collections at eye level to captivate your customers effectively. Keep jewelries organized with a forward-facing orientation on shelves. This not only maintains a tidy and appealing appearance but also makes it easy for customers to identify and try on the jewelries.

Create striking displays at strategic locations within your store to showcase seasonal jewelry collections, promotions, or high-margin products. Regularly update these displays to maintain customer engagement and curiosity.

Enhance customer convenience and stimulate cross-selling by grouping complementary jewelry styles together. For instance, positioning athletic jewelries alongside athletic accessories can encourage customers to complete their look.

Embrace the power of seasonal and holiday themes in your displays and signage. This creates a festive shopping atmosphere that resonates with your customers and encourages them to explore the latest seasonal jewelry offerings.

Ensure that each pair of jewelries is clearly labeled with pricing information and descriptions. Consider incorporating digital price tags for increased flexibility and pricing accuracy.

Dedicate specific sections of your store for promotional displays, featuring offers such as "buy one, get one free" or "jewelry of the week." This enhances their visibility and impact, prompting customers to take advantage of special deals. Strategically place small, high-margin jewelry accessories, like insoles or jewelry care products, near the checkout area. This encourages customers to make impromptu purchases, contributing to increased sales.

Implement efficient inventory rotation strategies, ensuring that older jewelry styles are prominently displayed and sold before newer arrivals. This proactive approach minimizes the risk of outdated merchandise, optimizing your store's product newness and reducing waste.

By implementing these tailored shelving and merchandising strategies, your jewelry store can create an enticing shopping environment that not only enhances the presentation of your products but also maximizes sales and customer satisfaction.

Equipment and Fixtures

Selecting the right equipment and fixtures is essential for ensuring the functionality and efficiency of your jewelry store. Here are key considerations:

Display Cases and Showcases: Choose high-quality and versatile display cases and showcases to exhibit your jewelry collections effectively. Opt for designs that highlight the elegance and uniqueness of your pieces while providing ample security.

Display Fixtures: Choose various fixtures like necklace stands, ring trays, earring racks, and bracelet holders to organize and present jewelry effectively.

Lighting Systems: Invest in suitable lighting systems that accentuate the brilliance and allure of your jewelry. Different types of lighting, such as spotlights or ambient lighting, can enhance the visual appeal of specific pieces.

Security Measures: Implement robust security measures, including surveillance cameras and alarm systems, to safeguard your valuable inventory. These systems not only deter theft but also provide crucial footage for security investigations.

Storage Solutions: Utilize efficient storage solutions to organize and store your jewelry inventory. Consider secure safes or vaults for high-value items and efficient storage cabinets for everyday pieces.

Point-of-Sale (POS) Systems: Install reliable POS systems equipped with barcode scanners and payment processing capabilities. These systems should seamlessly integrate with your inventory management software for smooth transactions and accurate stock tracking.

Cleaning and Maintenance Equipment: Acquire appropriate tools and equipment for cleaning and maintaining your jewelry displays and cases. This includes cleaning solutions, microfiber cloths, and specialized tools for intricate pieces.

Customer Comfort: Consider providing seating areas or comfortable spaces for customers to browse and try on jewelry comfortably. Creating a welcoming and relaxed environment encourages customers to spend more time exploring your collections.

Decorative Elements: Incorporate aesthetic elements such as decorative fixtures, artistic displays, or thematic designs that complement and elevate the overall ambiance of your store.

By carefully selecting these equipment and fixture elements, you can create a visually appealing, secure, and efficient environment that showcases your jewelry while ensuring a pleasant and engaging shopping experience for your customers.

Interior Design

Creating an inviting and functional interior design for a jewelry store is crucial for attracting customers, enhancing the shopping experience, and ultimately driving sales. The store's layout, decor, and ambiance play a significant role in setting the stage for showcasing your jewelry collections. Here are key aspects to consider when designing the interior of a jewelry store:

The layout of your jewelry store should be well-organized and easy to navigate. Consider an open floor plan with clearly defined sections for different jewelry categories, making it simple for customers to find what they're looking for. Adequate space planning ensures that aisles are wide enough for comfortable browsing, especially when customers want to try on jewelries.

Proper lighting is essential for highlighting your jewelry displays and creating an appealing atmosphere. A combination of natural and artificial lighting can be used to enhance the brightness of your store. Track lighting, spotlights, and LED strips can draw attention to specific jewelry collections, creating a visual focal point.

Selecting the right flooring is crucial. Durable and easy-to-clean materials are preferred, as jewelry stores often experience heavy foot traffic. Wooden or vinyl flooring can provide an upscale and comfortable feel, while polished concrete is a contemporary choice that complements various interior styles.

The type and design of shelving and displays have a significant impact on the presentation of your jewelry inventory. Consider sleek, modular shelving units that can be adjusted to accommodate different jewelry sizes and styles. Transparent acrylic or glass displays can add a touch of elegance while providing clear visibility of your products.

Incorporate your store's branding elements into the decor. This may include a distinctive color scheme, logos, and signage. Create a cohesive brand image that extends to your jewelry displays, wall art, and other decorative elements.

Provide comfortable seating areas where customers can try on jewelries. Placing strategically positioned mirrors near seating areas allows customers to assess the fit and appearance of the jewelries from different angles.

Consider the ambiance you want to create in your jewelry store. Music, whether it's soft and subtle or upbeat, can influence the shopping experience. Scent, if used, should be subtle and pleasant. Some stores also incorporate interactive elements or sensory experiences to engage customers.

Regularly update your jewelry displays to showcase new arrivals, seasonal collections, or promotions. Visual merchandising techniques, such as creating lifestyle displays or theme-based setups, can captivate customers and encourage them to explore your offerings.

Ensure that your store is accessible to all customers, including those with disabilities. This includes providing ramps, handrails, and wider aisles to accommodate wheelchair users and individuals with mobility challenges.

Use clear and informative signage throughout your store to help customers find specific jewelry categories or brands. Signage should be consistent with your store's branding and be positioned prominently.

Your store's design and layout should align with your brand identity and the preferences of your target audience. Continuously evaluate and refine your store's design based on customer feedback and changing market trends to create a shopping environment that keeps customers coming back.

The design and layout of your jewelry store are critical elements that influence customer experience, operational efficiency, and sales performance. By carefully considering store layout, shelving and merchandising strategies, equipment and fixtures, and interior design, you can create a shopping environment that attracts customers, encourages sales, and sets your jewelry store apart from the competition.

Chapter 6:
Product Selection and Suppliers

The success of your jewelry store heavily relies on the products you offer and the relationships you build with suppliers. In this chapter, we will delve into the critical aspects of product selection and suppliers, including building relationships with suppliers, managing inventory effectively, implementing pricing strategies, and considering private label products as part of your inventory.

Building Connections with Suppliers and Artisans

The people behind the pieces—your suppliers and artisans—are your behind-the-scenes heroes. They're the ones who ensure your jewelry isn't just beautiful but also top-notch in quality and craftsmanship.

It all starts with finding reliable suppliers who provide the good stuff—precious metals, gemstones, and all the things that make your jewelry shine. Networking, hitting up trade shows, and cruising online platforms specialized in jewelry supplies are great ways to link up with these trustworthy suppliers. But more than just finding them, it's about building that trust, knowing they're as dedicated to quality and ethical sourcing as you are.

For stores offering those one-of-a-kind, artisan-crafted pieces, connecting with talented craftsmen and women is key. It's not just about the jewelry; it's about the passion and skill behind each piece. Visiting their workshops, chatting, and really getting their creative vibe helps forge strong partnerships. Working closely with these artisans opens up possibilities for unique designs and that personal touch that makes your store stand out.

Once you've found your dream team of suppliers and artisans, it's all about nurturing those relationships. It's not just a business transaction; it's a partnership built on trust and respect. Keeping the communication open, sticking to agreements, and giving feedback helps solidify these connections. This way, you're ensuring a smooth flow of materials and creations, and it's a win-win for everyone.

In today's conscientious market, ethical sourcing is a big deal. Customers want to know the story behind their bling—the where and how it's made. Finding partners who share your ethical values ensures your store stands for something more than just beautiful jewelry. It's about trust and integrity that resonates with your customers.

Partnerships aren't all smooth sailing. There might be ups and downs—price changes, shifts in trends, or scaling up your business. Staying in touch with your suppliers and artisans, being flexible, and finding solutions together is what keeps everything running smoothly.

So, these connections you build with suppliers and artisans? They're the heart and soul of your jewelry store. Finding the right partners, nurturing those bonds, sticking to ethical values, and being adaptable sets the stage for a business that's not just about beautiful jewelry but also about trust, craftsmanship, and a shared vision.

Product Selection and Sourcing

Crafting a compelling collection of jewelry stands as a pivotal cornerstone in establishing a thriving jewelry store. Your array of offerings defines your store's identity, magnetizes your intended audience, and wields a substantial influence on the store's profitability. Here's a guide to consider when choosing and sourcing jewelry.

Before diving into the world of jewelry sourcing, remember your store's niche and the market you're targeting. Are you catering to customers seeking high-end, luxurious pieces, individuals attracted to handcrafted artisanal designs, or those looking for affordable yet elegant accessories? Understanding this niche helps direct your focus. While a niche is important, it's also prudent to present a diverse selection of jewelry styles—from rings, necklaces, earrings, and bracelets to distinctive statement pieces—to accommodate various customer tastes.

Priority should be given to the quality of the jewelry you source. Customers value craftsmanship, durability, and unique designs. It's crucial to stay in the loop with the latest trends and customer preferences in the jewelry realm. This involves attending trade shows, scouring fashion magazines, and staying tuned to online platforms. Such knowledge becomes the compass steering your choices in sourcing jewelry.

Diversification in sourcing becomes key for maintaining a versatile and reliable inventory. Considering multiple suppliers minimizes the risk of inventory shortages. It also allows room for negotiation, securing favorable terms and pricing across different suppliers. Whether you opt for local artisans or global manufacturers, weigh the benefits. Local sourcing may offer quick delivery and a chance to support local craft, while global connections provide access to diverse designs and competitive pricing.

Building relationships with wholesale suppliers or forging partnerships with jewelry manufacturers broadens your access to a wide spectrum of jewelry styles. This opens avenues for sourcing cost-effective inventory for your store.

If you're aiming for exclusivity, consider private labeling. Collaborating with manufacturers to craft and label your distinctive line of jewelry sets your store apart from competitors, adding a unique touch.

Managing inventory in tune with seasonal trends is vital. Consistency in jewelry availability throughout the year, complemented by seasonal variations, should be part of your strategy.

Quality control measures are imperative in ensuring the jewelry you receive meets the necessary standards. Vigorous inspections of incoming shipments become crucial, especially when sourcing globally.

With consumers increasingly valuing sustainability, consider sourcing from manufacturers with ethical and sustainable practices. Promoting eco-friendly jewelry aligns with this growing consumer preference, enhancing your brand image and appealing to environmentally conscious customers.

Establishing favorable terms with suppliers, be it pricing, minimum orders, delivery schedules, or return policies, is pivotal. Cultivating strong supplier relationships lays the groundwork for better deals and reliable partnerships.

Crafting an enticing jewelry collection and sourcing it effectively is a linchpin for your jewelry store's triumph. A well-curated inventory that aligns with your customer base's preferences and quality expectations, coupled with strategic sourcing practices, becomes the secret to standing out and securing lasting success in the competitive jewelry market.

Building Relationships with Suppliers

Building strong and lasting relationships with suppliers is a crucial aspect of running a successful jewelry store. These partnerships not only ensure a steady supply of products but also offer various benefits that can positively impact your business.

Firstly, effective communication is the foundation of any strong supplier relationship. Open and transparent lines of communication foster trust and understanding between you and your suppliers. Regularly discussing your needs, concerns, and expectations can lead to better collaboration and problem-solving when issues arise.

Another key element in building supplier relationships is reliability. Consistently meeting payment deadlines and honoring agreements demonstrates your commitment and reliability as a business partner. This reliability can lead to better terms, such as discounts, extended credit, or priority access to high-demand products.

Mutual respect is essential. Treating your suppliers with respect and professionalism, just as you expect from them, creates a positive working environment. This can lead to better customer service, faster response times, and a willingness to go the extra mile to support your store.

Building trust takes time and effort. One way to foster trust is by sharing your business plans and goals with your suppliers. When suppliers understand your vision, they can tailor their offerings and support to align with your objectives.

Collaboration is also key in supplier relationships. Engaging in joint initiatives, such as marketing campaigns or product development, can be mutually beneficial. This not only strengthens the bond but can also lead to innovative solutions and increased sales.

Regularly reviewing and evaluating your supplier relationships is vital. Assess the quality of products, delivery timelines, and the overall value they bring to your business. If issues arise, address them promptly and constructively, seeking solutions that benefit both parties.

Building relationships with suppliers is not just about transactions; it's about creating partnerships that benefit both your jewelry store and your suppliers. Open communication, reliability, mutual respect, trust, collaboration, and regular evaluation are the pillars of successful supplier relationships. Investing time and effort in nurturing these relationships can contribute significantly to your store's success and sustainability.

Pricing Strategies

Pricing strategy in the jewelry industry is quite the balancing act. It's not just about the cost of making a piece; it's about what customers are willing to pay for it, what the competition is doing, and how your jewelry is perceived in the market.

One way to price jewelry is by looking at the production cost and then adding a markup. This method, called cost-based pricing, considers everything that goes into making the piece – materials, labor, overheads – and then tacks on an extra percentage to set the selling price. But sometimes, this approach overlooks what customers are willing to pay based on how they see the value of the jewelry.

That's where value-based pricing comes in. This strategy focuses on what customers believe the jewelry is worth, rather than just the production cost. Things like unique designs, rare materials, top-notch craftsmanship, or a brand's reputation all contribute to how customers perceive the value of a piece. And often, this perceived value is much higher than the production cost.

Another way to decide on prices is by looking at the market. Market-based pricing involves checking out what competitors are charging and then setting your prices accordingly. It's about staying competitive but making sure you're making a profit too.

Then there's premium pricing, which is all about setting higher prices to give off that luxury vibe. It's for those brands that want to position themselves as exclusive – offering something that's not just a piece of jewelry but a symbol of luxury and prestige.

On the flip side, there's discount pricing. This strategy appeals to customers looking for a bargain. Offering discounts or running sales can attract those who are more price-conscious. But you've got to be careful with this one – you don't want to make your jewelry seem less valuable.

Technology has also opened up dynamic pricing, where you can adjust prices on the fly based on what's happening in the market. It's all about responding to changes in demand, stock levels, or even how customers are behaving.

When figuring out prices, it's not just about the numbers; it's also about psychology. Prices like $99.99 instead of $100 might seem cheaper, even if it's just a cent difference. Plus, adding extra services or bundling items can make the deal seem sweeter without changing the base price.

Different customers also have different ideas about what they're willing to pay. Tailoring prices for various customer groups, like luxury buyers or trend-chasers, can be a smart move.

In the end, deciding on how to price jewelry is a mix of considering costs, understanding what customers see as valuable, keeping an eye on the competition, and sometimes, even playing with psychology a bit. It's all about finding that sweet spot where your jewelry is both attractive to customers and profitable for your business.

Chapter 7:
Staffing and Management

Effective staffing and management are fundamental to the success of your jewelry store. In this chapter, we will explore the key components of staffing and managing your jewelry store, including the hiring and training of employees, the creation of employee policies, scheduling and shift management, and performance evaluation.

Staff Needed

Staffing a jewelry store effectively is crucial for providing excellent customer service, maintaining operations, and achieving overall success. Here are the key positions and roles you should consider when assembling your staff:

Sales Associates: These individuals are the face of the store, engaging with customers, showcasing jewelry pieces, and offering guidance on selections. They should possess excellent communication skills, product knowledge, and the ability to assist customers in finding the perfect piece.

Jewelry Specialists: A team of experts well-versed in gemology, jewelry design, and the various types of metals and stones is essential. They can offer in-depth knowledge and guidance, especially for customers seeking detailed information or looking for custom-made pieces.

Store Manager: Responsible for overseeing daily operations, managing staff, ensuring sales targets are met, and maintaining the store's overall efficiency. They also handle inventory, customer service, and implement strategies to boost sales.

Customer Service Representatives: These staff members handle inquiries, assist with purchases, process transactions, and manage customer concerns or complaints. Exceptional interpersonal skills and a customer-centric approach are crucial in this role.

Jewelry Repair and Maintenance Specialists: Having professionals who can offer repair services or maintenance advice for jewelry pieces is beneficial. Their expertise ensures that customers' treasured pieces are well taken care of and restored to their original beauty.

Security Personnel: To safeguard high-value items and ensure the safety of both customers and staff, having security personnel or surveillance systems in place is essential.

Online Sales and E-commerce Experts: With the increasing trend of online shopping, having staff knowledgeable in managing the store's online presence, handling e-commerce operations, and engaging customers through digital platforms is becoming increasingly important.

When hiring staff for a jewelry store, it's vital to prioritize qualities such as professionalism, trustworthiness, strong communication skills, and a passion for jewelry. A team that not only possesses product knowledge but also understands the emotional significance of jewelry purchases can greatly enhance the overall shopping experience for customers. Training programs and continuous education in gemology, customer service, and sales techniques can further develop staff expertise, ensuring they stay updated with industry trends and are equipped to cater to customers' needs effectively.

Hiring and Training Employees

The process of hiring and training employees is a critical foundation for your jewelry store's success. It begins with a well-planned recruitment process aimed at attracting candidates who align with your store's values and customer service standards. Utilizing various channels such as online job boards, local newspapers, and social media, you can advertise job openings effectively. Additionally, consider hosting in-person or virtual job fairs to engage potential candidates.

Once you've identified suitable candidates, a rigorous selection process, including resume screening, interviews, reference checks, and skills assessments, ensures that you select employees who not only possess the necessary qualifications but also fit well within your store's culture. Following the hiring process, invest in comprehensive training programs that encompass on-the-job training and formal training sessions. These programs ensure that your staff members are well-versed in product offerings, customer service expectations, safety protocols, and store policies.

Furthermore, emphasize the significance of customer service training as it is paramount in the jewelry industry. Equipping your staff with exceptional customer service skills, effective communication abilities, problem-solving capabilities, and conflict resolution techniques is essential. To maintain a consistent commitment to safety, implement safety training protocols, including proper equipment handling, sanitation practices, and emergency procedures. Finally, encourage continuous learning and development among your staff by offering opportunities for ongoing training, skill enhancement, and cross-training in multiple roles within the store.

Creating Employee Policies

Establishing clear and comprehensive employee policies is essential to maintaining a well-organized and harmonious work environment. Begin by developing an employee handbook that serves as a centralized resource for your staff, outlining the store's policies and procedures. Within this handbook, provide detailed information on work schedules, dress code expectations, attendance requirements, and performance expectations.

Additionally, articulate a code of conduct that sets forth expected behavior, ethical standards, and professional conduct for all employees. Emphasize the importance of respecting both customers and colleagues. Implement anti-discrimination and harassment policies to create a safe and inclusive workplace, complete with clear reporting procedures to ensure all employees are aware of their rights and protections.

Safety and health policies should be a top priority, addressing compliance with local regulations and conveying the importance of maintaining a safe work environment. In terms of compensation, offer transparency by detailing the compensation structure, benefits, and perks available to employees, including wage rates, overtime policies, and benefits programs. Equally important is defining expectations for attendance and punctuality, with guidelines on requesting time off, reporting absences, and addressing tardiness.

Moreover, create policies that facilitate conflict resolution, including a fair and confidential process for employees to address issues with management or colleagues. Finally, educate employees about the significance of respecting customer privacy and confidentiality, ensuring they understand the proper handling of sensitive information.

Scheduling and Shift Management

Efficient scheduling and shift management are vital components of jewelry store operations. To ensure optimal staffing levels, begin by determining the appropriate number of employees based on store traffic patterns, sales forecasts, and customer needs. Adjust staffing levels as needed during peak and off-peak hours to enhance customer service.

To streamline the scheduling process, utilize scheduling software or tools that consider employee availability, preferences, and labor laws when generating schedules. Offer flexibility in scheduling to accommodate employees' personal commitments and preferences, which can significantly boost morale and retention. Effective shift management is crucial, and overlapping shifts during busy hours can provide the necessary coverage for smooth operations.

Maintain open communication with employees concerning their schedules, promptly notifying them of any changes or updates. Consider implementing digital communication tools for efficient schedule distribution. To ensure compliance with labor laws, monitor and manage overtime effectively, which includes maintaining accurate records and adhering to overtime pay regulations. Equally important is providing adequate break and rest periods for employees, ensuring that designated break areas are easily accessible.

Performance Evaluation

Performance evaluation is a pivotal aspect of managing your jewelry store staff. Define key performance metrics for various roles within the store, including sales targets, customer service ratings, and productivity goals. Provide ongoing feedback to employees, helping them understand their strengths and areas for improvement. Encourage open dialogue and constructive feedback as part of your organizational culture.

Conduct regular performance reviews or evaluations to assess employee performance against established metrics and goals. Set aside dedicated time for these evaluations and involve employees in goal setting to align their individual objectives with the store's overall objectives. Recognize and reward outstanding performance through incentive programs, awards, or bonuses to motivate and retain high-performing employees.

Moreover, discuss career development opportunities with employees and provide guidance on how they can advance within the organization. Offer training and support for career growth, demonstrating your commitment to their professional development. In cases where employees are not meeting performance expectations, develop performance improvement plans that outline specific steps for improvement. Offer support and resources to help employees succeed while also being prepared to take appropriate action, including termination, if performance issues persist despite efforts to address them.

Managing staffing and employee performance is an ongoing process that demands attention to detail, effective communication, and a commitment to fostering a positive work environment. By hiring and training employees effectively, creating clear policies, managing schedules efficiently, and conducting performance evaluations, you can build a motivated and capable team that contributes significantly to the success of your jewelry store.

Chapter 8:
Marketing and Promotion

A well-crafted marketing and promotion strategy is essential to attract and retain customers, create a strong brand presence, and drive sales. In this chapter, we will explore the key components of effective marketing and promotion for your jewelry store, including developing a marketing plan, establishing your store's branding and image, implementing advertising and promotion strategies, and utilizing loyalty programs to foster customer loyalty and engagement.

Developing a Marketing Plan

A marketing plan serves as the guiding blueprint for a jewelry store's promotional activities, providing a structured approach to achieving desired outcomes. To develop a comprehensive marketing plan, several key steps should be followed.

Firstly, it's essential to establish clear and specific marketing objectives that adhere to the SMART criteria—objectives that are specific, measurable, achievable, relevant, and time-bound. These objectives may encompass goals such as increasing sales, expanding market share, or launching a new store location.

Understanding the target audience is equally critical. By creating detailed buyer personas, including demographic information, preferences, and behaviors, a jewelry store can tailor its marketing efforts effectively to resonate with its ideal customers.

Conducting a competitor analysis is another vital component. By scrutinizing the marketing strategies of competitors, a jewelry store can uncover opportunities for differentiation and gain insights into their strengths and weaknesses, enabling the development of a competitive advantage.

A well-defined marketing budget should be determined based on the store's objectives and available resources. This budget should be allocated across various marketing channels, including digital advertising, print media, social media, and in-store promotions, to maximize effectiveness.

The marketing mix, often represented by the four Ps (product, price, place, and promotion), must be carefully defined. This includes outlining product offerings, pricing strategies, distribution channels, and promotional tactics.

Developing a content strategy is pivotal for engaging and educating the audience. The plan should encompass the type of content to be produced, including blog posts, social media updates, email newsletters, and product guides.

Selecting the most appropriate marketing channels to reach the target audience is crucial. It involves considering a mix of online and offline channels, such as social media, email marketing, search engine optimization (SEO), pay-per-click (PPC) advertising, print media, and participation in local events.

Creating an implementation timeline is essential. This timeline should specify when each marketing initiative will be executed, ensuring alignment with the store's sales cycles and seasonal trends.

Measuring success is an integral part of the plan. Key performance indicators (KPIs) should be defined to gauge the effectiveness of marketing efforts. Tracking metrics such as website traffic, conversion rates, sales revenue, and customer acquisition cost provides valuable insights.

Finally, regular review and adjustment are vital for maintaining a dynamic marketing plan. Continuous monitoring and evaluation allow for data-driven decision-making and the flexibility to adapt strategies based on evolving circumstances and insights gained over time.

Branding and Store Image

Branding encompasses more than just a logo and a catchy slogan; it represents the essence of your jewelry store's identity. Building a strong brand image is not only essential for setting your store apart from competitors but also for fostering customer trust and leaving a lasting impression. To create a compelling brand identity, follow these essential steps:

Define Your Brand: The process begins by clearly defining your store's values, mission, and vision. What is it that you want your jewelry store to stand for, and what unique qualities will distinguish it from others in the market?

Logo and Visual Identity: Craft a memorable logo and visual identity that align with your brand's personality and values. It's crucial to ensure consistency in these branding elements across all marketing materials and in-store signage.

Store Layout and Design: The interior design and layout of your store should seamlessly align with your brand image. The atmosphere, color schemes, and decor should vividly convey your brand's values and resonate with your target audience.

Customer Experience: Delivering a consistent and exceptional customer experience is pivotal to upholding your brand promise. Train your staff to embody your brand values in their interactions with customers, creating a lasting impression.

Brand Messaging: Develop compelling brand messaging that effectively communicates your store's unique selling points and resonates with your intended audience. Maintain the consistency of this messaging across all communication channels.

Brand Voice: Cultivate a consistent brand voice that reflects your brand's personality. Whether it's a friendly, informative, or humorous tone, ensure that it remains aligned with your brand image.

Community Engagement: Actively engage with the local community and support causes that align with your brand values. Sponsoring local events, participating in charity initiatives, or contributing to environmental efforts can enhance your brand's reputation and foster a sense of community.

Feedback and Adaptation: Continuously seek feedback from your customers to gain insights into their perceptions of your brand. Be willing to adapt and evolve your brand identity in response to changing customer preferences and market trends.

In essence, branding and store image creation involve a holistic approach that encompasses visual identity, messaging, atmosphere, and customer experience. By meticulously crafting and nurturing your brand, you can establish a distinct and memorable identity in the jewelry market, leading to increased customer loyalty and trust.

Marketing and Advertising

Marketing and advertising are indispensable components of promoting your jewelry store and reaching your target audience effectively. These strategies encompass a range of activities and techniques aimed at boosting brand visibility, attracting customers, and nurturing their loyalty. Here's a detailed exploration of key elements within marketing and advertising for your jewelry store:

Targeted Marketing: To maximize the impact of your efforts, it's crucial to tailor your marketing activities to reach specific demographics and customer segments. By leveraging market research and customer data, you can identify your ideal audience, enabling you to create more precise and impactful marketing campaigns.

Digital Marketing: In the digital age, online advertising plays a pivotal role. This includes search engine optimization (SEO) to enhance your store's visibility on search engines, pay-per-click (PPC) advertising to target potential customers with specific ads, and social media marketing to engage with your audience and promote special offers.

Content Marketing: Developing high-quality, informative content that resonates with your target audience is a powerful strategy. Content can take various forms, including blog posts, videos, infographics, and product guides. By providing valuable information, you not only serve your customers but also establish your store as an authority in the jewelry industry.

Email Marketing: An effective email marketing strategy ensures that your customers stay informed about promotions, new arrivals, and special events. Personalizing your emails can improve engagement and customer retention.

Loyalty Programs: Implementing loyalty programs is a proven way to reward repeat customers. These programs may include discounts, points systems, or exclusive offers that incentivize shoppers to return to your store.

In-Store Promotions: Conducting in-store promotions, such as "buy one, get one free" offers, discounts, or product bundling, can be highly effective. Utilizing eye-catching signage and endcap displays can draw attention to these promotions.

Seasonal and Holiday Campaigns: Seasonal and holiday trends offer opportunities for themed campaigns and special promotions. This can encompass festive decorations, unique product offerings, and special events held within your store.

Community Engagement: Actively engaging with the local community through sponsorships, partnerships, and participation in local events can enhance your store's reputation and create a sense of community. Supporting local causes can be a meaningful way to connect with your customers.

Cross-Promotions: Collaborating with complementary businesses for cross-promotions can expand your reach. For instance, partnering with a local fashion stores to offer discounts when customers purchase both clothes and jewelries can benefit both businesses.

Customer Reviews and Testimonials: Encouraging satisfied customers to leave reviews and testimonials online can significantly impact your store's reputation and attract new customers.

Mobile Advertising: Given the growing number of shoppers using smartphones for shopping, optimizing your online presence for mobile users is crucial. This includes ensuring that your website is mobile-friendly and considering mobile advertising options.

Measurement and Analysis: Continuous monitoring of your marketing and advertising efforts is essential. Analyzing data, tracking key performance indicators (KPIs), and adjusting your strategies based on insights from customer behavior and campaign results are crucial for ongoing success.

Incorporating these diverse techniques and maintaining an adaptable approach to marketing and advertising can help your jewelry store create a compelling and memorable shopping experience while driving growth and profitability.

Chapter 9:
Operations and Logistics

Efficient operations and logistics are the backbone of a successful jewelry store. In this chapter, we will explore the intricacies of managing daily store operations, optimizing supply chain management, controlling inventory, and ensuring quality assurance to deliver a seamless shopping experience to your customers.

Daily Store Operations

Running a successful jewelry store involves a multitude of daily tasks and responsibilities that demand meticulous planning and execution. These operational processes are the backbone of the store's efficiency and customer satisfaction. Here's an overview of essential daily store operations:

Store Opening and Closing: Establishing clear opening and closing procedures is paramount to ensuring the seamless commencement and conclusion of each business day. These procedures encompass tasks such as securely unlocking and locking the premises, setting up enticing displays, and conducting closing inventory counts to maintain inventory accuracy.

Staff Scheduling: Crafting a well-structured daily staff schedule is critical for maintaining optimal staffing levels, especially during peak business hours. Efficient allocation of staff resources not only guarantees excellent customer service but also minimizes labor costs, contributing to overall operational effectiveness.

Customer Service: Prioritize customer service excellence by providing extensive training to your staff. This training should encompass welcoming and assisting customers, addressing their inquiries promptly, and ensuring a consistently pleasant shopping experience that fosters customer loyalty.

Checkout Process: Streamlining the checkout process is essential to minimize waiting times for customers. Implement efficient point-of-sale (POS) systems and provide comprehensive training to cashiers to facilitate swift and accurate transaction processing, enhancing customer satisfaction.

Store Maintenance: Regularly inspecting and maintaining the store's physical premises is crucial. This entails tasks such as routine cleaning, equipment maintenance, and promptly addressing any safety hazards to create a safe and pleasant shopping environment.

Merchandising: Ensuring that products are displayed attractively and that shelves remain well-stocked is pivotal in maximizing sales and customer engagement. Frequent restocking and strategic visual merchandising contribute to a dynamic and enticing shopping experience.

Order Fulfillment: If your store offers online and phone orders, it's imperative to efficiently manage order fulfillment. Timely processing and delivery or pickup of customer orders are essential for ensuring high levels of customer satisfaction and repeat business.

Security: Implementing comprehensive security measures, including surveillance cameras, alarms, and loss prevention strategies, is vital to protect against theft and to ensure the safety of both customers and employees. A secure shopping environment enhances customer trust.

In conclusion, the daily operations of a jewelry store are multifaceted and intricately interconnected. Effective management of these operations is pivotal in providing outstanding customer experiences, maintaining store efficiency, and ensuring the overall success of the business.

Supply Chain Management

Supply chain management plays a crucial role in the efficient and effective operation of a jewelry store. It involves the planning, coordination, and control of the flow of goods and information from suppliers to the store's shelves, with the ultimate goal of meeting customer demand while minimizing costs and maximizing profitability.

One of the key aspects of supply chain management for a jewelry store is vendor selection and management. Choosing reliable and cost-effective suppliers is essential to ensure a steady and high-quality supply of products. Jewelry stores often work with a variety of suppliers, including artisans, wholesalers, and distributors, to source new items. Establishing strong relationships with these suppliers can lead to better pricing, timely deliveries, and access to unique products that can give the store a competitive edge.

Inventory management is another critical component of supply chain management for a jewelry store. Balancing inventory levels to meet customer demand while avoiding overstocking or understocking is a delicate task. Advanced inventory management systems and technologies can help store managers track product levels in real-time, forecast demand, and automatically reorder products when necessary. This reduces the risk of product damage, stockouts, and excess inventory, which can eat into profits. We will delve deeper into this next.

Efficient transportation and logistics are vital for ensuring that products move smoothly from suppliers to the jewelry store's shelves. Jewelry stores often have multiple distribution centers to receive and distribute products to individual store locations. Optimizing routes, scheduling deliveries, and using technology like GPS tracking can help reduce transportation costs and ensure on-time deliveries. Moreover, eco-friendly transportation practices can align with sustainability goals and reduce the store's carbon footprint.

In today's highly competitive retail landscape, data analytics and technology play an increasingly significant role in supply chain management for jewelry stores. Collecting and analyzing data on customer preferences, sales trends, and inventory turnover can help stores make informed decisions about product assortment, pricing, and promotions. The use of RFID tags, barcodes, and advanced software systems can enhance inventory visibility, reduce errors, and streamline the replenishment process.

Effective supply chain management is essential for the success of a jewelry store. It involves vendor selection, inventory management, transportation, technology and data analytics. By optimizing these aspects of the supply chain, jewelry stores can enhance customer satisfaction, reduce costs, and remain competitive in a dynamic and evolving retail industry.

Inventory Management

Inventory control is a crucial element of supply chain management that plays a pivotal role in various industries. It refers to the processes and strategies utilized by organizations to efficiently manage their stock of goods. Effective inventory control is essential for ensuring product availability, reducing carrying costs, avoiding stockouts, and optimizing overall business operations.

One of the primary objectives of inventory control is to find the right equilibrium between maintaining sufficient stock levels to meet customer demand and minimizing excess inventory.

Excessive inventory can tie up valuable capital and storage space, increasing the risks of obsolescence and damage. Conversely, insufficient inventory can lead to stockouts, resulting in lost sales and customer dissatisfaction. Businesses employ inventory control methods to determine optimal stock levels for each product, relying on historical sales data, demand forecasts, and lead times.

Accurate and up-to-date record-keeping is fundamental to effective inventory control. This entails tracking the quantity, value, location, and movements of every item in the inventory. Modern businesses often utilize computerized inventory management systems that automate these tasks, offering real-time visibility into stock levels and facilitating rapid decision-making. These systems can generate reports on stock turnover rates, reorder points, and supplier performance, facilitating inventory control efforts.

The ABC analysis is a fundamental concept in inventory control, classifying products into categories based on their significance and value. "A" items represent high-value, high-priority products requiring meticulous monitoring and tighter control. "B" items hold moderate importance, while "C" items are low-value, low-priority products. This categorization enables businesses to allocate resources effectively, focusing efforts on managing the most critical items.

Inventory control strategies encompass various techniques for managing demand fluctuations and uncertainties. Safety stock, for instance, involves maintaining a buffer of extra inventory to account for unexpected demand surges or supply delays. Reorder points and economic order quantity (EOQ) calculations help determine when to reorder products to maintain desired stock levels while minimizing carrying costs. Just-in-time (JIT) inventory systems take an alternative approach, aiming to minimize inventory holding costs by receiving goods from suppliers precisely when needed.

Effective inventory control yields numerous benefits for businesses. It can reduce carrying costs associated with storage, insurance, and handling. It helps prevent overstocking, which ties up capital, and understocking, which results in missed sales opportunities. Furthermore, it contributes to stronger supplier relationships by providing accurate demand forecasts and ensuring timely replenishment orders.

Inventory control is an indispensable practice within supply chain management, aimed at striking a balance between optimal stock levels and minimal carrying costs. It involves the application of techniques such as ABC analysis, safety stock, EOQ, and JIT to streamline inventory management. By implementing effective inventory control strategies, businesses can enhance their overall efficiency, customer satisfaction, and financial performance.

Quality Assurance

Ensuring the quality of the jewelry you receive from suppliers is crucial for your store's reputation. To start, clearly outline the standards you expect and share these with your suppliers. When shipments arrive, begin by checking the packaging for any signs of damage or potential issues.

After that, take a close look at each piece of jewelry. Inspect for any flaws like scratches, dents, or irregularities in the gemstones or metalwork. The overall finish should align with the quality you promise your customers.

Confirm the authenticity of the materials used. Sometimes, you may need to perform tests or use specific tools to verify the purity of metals and the genuineness of gemstones. This assurance builds trust with your clientele.

Pay attention to sizing, particularly for items like rings and bracelets. Accurate sizing is vital to prevent customer dissatisfaction.

Examine any moving parts or closures on the jewelry pieces. They should function smoothly and securely to ensure customer satisfaction.

If you encounter any issues, document them and promptly inform your supplier. Having clear procedures for handling returns or replacements for subpar items is essential.

Maintain detailed records of your inspections. This practice enables you to spot any recurring quality issues and make informed decisions about future orders and supplier relationships.

Consistently refining and updating your quality assessment procedures will enable you to deliver high-quality jewelry consistently, fostering customer loyalty and trust in your store.
Efficient operations and logistics, coupled with a strong focus on quality assurance, are essential for the success and sustainability of your jewelry store. By carefully managing daily operations, optimizing your supply chain, controlling inventory, and ensuring product quality, you can provide a seamless shopping experience that keeps customers coming back.

Chapter 10:
Growth and Expansion

Expanding your jewelry store business is a significant step toward increasing profitability and market presence. In this chapter, we'll explore various strategies for growth and expansion, including broadening your product line, opening additional locations, considering franchising opportunities, and exploring international expansion.

Expanding Your Product Line

Diversifying your product offerings can breathe new life into your jewelry store and attract a broader customer base. Here's how to approach expanding your product line:

Market Research: To begin, conduct thorough market research to identify products in demand within your community. This step involves considering customer surveys, analyzing market trends, and assessing competitor offerings. By understanding what your customers want and what's currently popular, you can make informed decisions about which products to add to your inventory.

Supplier Relationships: Strengthening your relationships with existing suppliers is crucial, and also seek out new ones to source the additional products you plan to offer. Building strong supplier partnerships ensures a consistent and reliable supply of new items, helping you maintain the quality and availability of your expanded product line.

Inventory Management: As you expand your product line, it's essential to revise your inventory management strategies. This includes reevaluating your storage capacity, shelving layouts, and tracking systems. Adequate storage and efficient organization are key to managing a more diverse inventory effectively.

Training and Staffing: Your employees play a vital role in the success of your expanded product line. Ensure your staff is knowledgeable about the new products and can assist customers with inquiries. Consider providing specialized training where necessary to enhance their expertise and confidence when dealing with the new offerings.

Marketing and Promotion: Creating effective marketing campaigns is crucial to introducing the new products to your customer base. Utilize a mix of strategies, including in-store displays, digital advertising, and promotional events, to generate interest and inform your customers about the exciting additions to your inventory.

Customer Feedback: Once the new products are on the shelves, continuously gather customer feedback. This valuable input allows you to fine-tune your offerings and make adjustments based on customer preferences. Listening to your customers and responding to their needs helps ensure the long-term success of your expanded product line.

In summary, expanding your product line can be a strategic move to grow your jewelry store business. However, it should be approached systematically, with careful consideration of market research, supplier relationships, inventory management, employee training, marketing efforts, and ongoing customer feedback. By following these steps, you can effectively diversify your product offerings and attract a wider customer base while maintaining customer satisfaction and profitability.

Opening Additional Locations

Expanding your jewelry store by opening additional locations can significantly increase your reach and market share. However, this endeavor involves a series of crucial considerations to ensure a successful expansion.

Location Selection: One of the most critical factors in opening new jewelry store locations is selecting the right spot. Conduct thorough location analysis to identify areas with high foot traffic, underserved markets, or demographics that align with your target customer base. Understanding the local market dynamics and competition is essential in making an informed decision.

Legal and Regulatory Requirements: Before proceeding with a new location, it's vital to navigate the legal and regulatory landscape. Ensure you understand and comply with local zoning laws, permits, and regulations specific to the jewelry retail industry. Failing to do so can lead to costly delays and complications.

Financial Planning: Create a comprehensive financial plan for the new location. This plan should include detailed projections of startup costs, operating expenses, and revenue expectations. Securing the necessary financing or capital to fund the expansion is essential to ensure a smooth launch and sustained growth.

Staffing: The success of a new store often hinges on the quality and readiness of your staff. Begin the hiring and training process well in advance of the opening to ensure that the team is adequately prepared to serve customers and manage operations. Consistency in service quality across all locations is key to maintaining your brand's reputation.

Supply Chain Management: Expanding to additional locations requires a reevaluation of your supply chain and logistics operations. Consider centralizing warehousing and distribution to ensure consistent product availability across all stores. Efficient supply chain management is crucial for minimizing costs and ensuring product freshness.

Marketing and Branding: Developing a solid marketing strategy is essential to introduce the new location to the community. Leverage your existing brand identity, but be prepared to customize it to the local market. Tailoring your marketing efforts to reflect the unique characteristics and preferences of the new location can help build a loyal customer base.

Monitoring and Evaluation: After opening, continuously monitor the performance of the new location. Establish key performance indicators (KPIs) to assess its success and compare it to your initial projections. Be prepared to make adjustments to operations, marketing, and staffing based on the data and feedback received to ensure the ongoing success of the new store.

In conclusion, opening additional locations for your jewelry store can be a rewarding strategy for growth, but it requires careful planning and execution. By addressing location selection, legal requirements, financial planning, staffing, supply chain management, marketing, and ongoing evaluation, you can increase your chances of a successful expansion and enhance your market presence.

Franchising Opportunities

Franchising opportunities offer a unique avenue for business expansion and growth. This business model allows entrepreneurs to replicate a successful and established brand, concept, or product by licensing the rights to operate under the parent company's name and guidance. Here, we delve into the key aspects of franchising opportunities.

One of the primary advantages of franchising is the ability to tap into a proven business model. Franchisors typically have a track record of success, a well-developed business plan, and a strong brand identity. This can reduce the risks associated with starting a new business from scratch and increase the likelihood of profitability.

For entrepreneurs, franchising offers a level of independence while still benefiting from the support and resources of an established brand. Franchisees can leverage the franchisor's expertise in areas such as marketing, operations, and supply chain management. This support can be especially beneficial for individuals who may have limited experience in running a business.

Franchising opportunities also come with a ready-made customer base. Established brands often have a loyal following, which can translate into a steady stream of customers from day one. This can significantly reduce the time and effort required to build brand recognition and attract customers.

However, it's crucial for potential franchisees to carefully evaluate the terms and conditions of the franchise agreement. Franchise agreements outline the responsibilities and obligations of both the franchisor and the franchisee. These agreements often include details about fees, royalties, territorial restrictions, and operational standards. Prospective franchisees should seek legal and financial advice to ensure they fully understand the terms before committing.

Franchising opportunities extend to various industries, from fast food and retail to fitness centers and retail businesses. The choice of franchise should align with the interests, skills, and financial capacity of the potential franchisee. Conducting thorough market research and due diligence is essential to select the right franchise that matches one's goals and resources.

Once a franchise is established, ongoing communication and collaboration between the franchisor and franchisee are critical. Franchisees benefit from regular training, updates on best practices, and support in addressing operational challenges. Franchisors, in turn, rely on franchisees to maintain the brand's reputation and uphold quality standards.

In conclusion, franchising opportunities provide a pathway for entrepreneurs to enter the business world with the backing of an established brand and support structure. It offers a balance between independence and guidance, making it an appealing option for those looking to start their own businesses. However, due diligence and a clear understanding of the franchise agreement are essential to ensure a successful and mutually beneficial partnership between franchisor and franchisee.

Each of these growth and expansion strategies comes with its own set of opportunities and challenges. The choice of which path to pursue should align with your business goals, resources, and risk tolerance. Careful planning, market research, and a commitment to maintaining the quality and values of your jewelry store are essential elements of successful growth and expansion in the highly competitive jewelry industry.

Conclusion

Starting and running a successful jewelry store is a challenging but rewarding endeavor. In this comprehensive guide, we have explored every facet of this journey, from the initial considerations of why to start a jewelry store and whether it's the right fit for you, to the intricate details of market research, legal considerations, financing, store design, staffing, marketing, operations, and various expansion strategies.

The jewelry store industry is a dynamic and competitive one, marked by changing consumer preferences, evolving technologies, and shifting market trends. To thrive in this environment, you must be adaptable, customer-focused, and committed to delivering a top-notch shopping experience.

Key takeaways from this guide include:

Understanding Your Market: Thorough market research is the foundation of your jewelry store's success. Knowing your target audience, competition, and location dynamics will guide your business decisions.

Legal and Regulatory Compliance: Navigating the legal and regulatory landscape is crucial. Choosing the right business structure, obtaining permits, and ensuring health and safety compliance are non-negotiable steps.

Financing and Budgeting: Carefully estimate your startup costs, secure funding, and manage your finances diligently. Budgeting and financial planning are essential for long-term sustainability.

Store Design and Layout: A well-designed store layout, effective shelving, and attractive merchandising contribute to a pleasant shopping experience that keeps customers coming back.

Product Selection and Suppliers: Building strong relationships with suppliers, managing inventory efficiently, setting competitive prices, and exploring private label options are key to product selection and procurement.

Staffing and Management: Hiring and training a motivated team, establishing employee policies, efficient scheduling, and performance evaluation are essential for smooth store operations.

Marketing and Promotion: Developing a comprehensive marketing plan, building a strong brand image, implementing effective advertising strategies, and utilizing loyalty programs are vital for attracting and retaining customers.

Operations and Logistics: Managing daily store operations, optimizing supply chain management, controlling inventory, and maintaining quality assurance are the cornerstones of a well-run jewelry store.

Growth and Expansion: Strategies such as expanding your product line, opening additional locations, exploring franchising opportunities, and venturing into international markets offer avenues for growth and expansion.

In the jewelry store business, customer satisfaction is paramount. By providing a wide variety of quality products, exceptional service, and a seamless shopping experience, you can build a loyal customer base and position your store for long-term success.

Remember that success in the jewelry industry requires ongoing adaptability, a commitment to innovation, and a dedication to maintaining the highest standards of quality and customer service. As you embark on this journey, may this guide serve as a valuable resource to help you navigate the challenges and seize the opportunities that come your way in the world of jewelry retail. Best of luck on your path to building a thriving jewelry store business.